Beginning Activities for English Language Learners

Lee Colman

National Textbook Company
a division of *NTC Publishing Group* • Lincolnwood, Illinois USA

To the teacher:
 The blackline masters in this book are designed to be photocopied for classroom use only.

1992 Printing

Published by National Textbook Company, a division of NTC Publishing Group,
© 1992, 1987 by NTC Publishing Group, 4255 West Touhy Avenue,
Lincolnwood (Chicago), Illinois 60646-1975 USA.
2 3 4 5 6 7 8 9 0 ML 9 8 7 6 5 4 3 2

To Jeannette and Serge Rousseau,
my first ESL students and now my loving friends.

Acknowledgments

The author wishes to express her gratitude to the students listed below for their splendid contributions, creative efforts, and enthusiasm; to Marian Shields Colman, a talented illustrator; to William Pugliese for his endless encouragement and copying assistance; to June Zuccarini, a typist-editor par excellence; to Maurine Hoffman, whose help with the final copy and valued advice were essential to the book; to Michael Ross and Becky Rauff, my superb editors; and last, but not least, to Fairfield University for the opportunity to work in a milieu which enhances creativity and teacher development.

Contributors:
Judith A. Baxter
Maureen E. Brown
Rosemary M. Dellinger
Shawn Dunham
Sue W. Eckert
Leigh J. Gray
Yi-Ti Ma
Anne Marie McEvoy
Lisa B. Nickerson
Amy J. Richards
Laura Kay Zavesky

Contents

Introduction

This collection of activities and accompanying blackline masters is the ideal resource for teachers of English to nonnative or remedial students at the beginning level. Each activity is designed to aid in teaching an aspect of the English language while making use of a particular learning style. Teachers will appreciate the easy-to-use format of the book; each activity is outlined in lesson plan form, with the rationale, objectives, materials needed, and procedure for performing the activity carefully noted. Most of the activities involve the use of worksheets, picture cards, etc., which are provided on blackline masters. For convenience, the lesson plans appear as a group at the front of the book, followed by the blackline masters. Each master is number-keyed to the appropriate lesson plan.

The activities in this book are organized according to learning styles, a concept which recognizes the fact that different students learn in different ways. By taking advantage of students' natural learning styles, teachers can enhance the English language learning experience.

Descriptions of the twelve basic learning styles appear on pages ix–xi. The material in these profiles was originally studied and gathered by Thomas de Tullio. It draws on the work of other psychologists and psycholinguists, including Herman Witkin, Leona Tyler, G. S. Klein, P. S. Holz-man, J. P. Guilford, D. R. Goodenough, R. W. Gardner, P. Vernon, N. Kogan, and J. Kagan.

Defining learning styles is a complex problem. Each one has distinctive characteristics; however, some characteristics are common to more than one style. As a result, the teacher must look for combinations of characteristics in order to determine which learning style is best suited to a particular student or class. Moreover, as students mature, they tend to adopt new learning styles; thus, adults often exhibit properties of most of the styles.

The activities in this book can be used in a number of ways. Selecting activities that make use of the students' natural learning style(s) will allow students to relax and absorb new material in a comfortable, familiar way. On the other hand, new learning styles can be introduced to develop desired characteristics, thus expanding the students' capacity for learning. Most of the activities can be easily adapted for use by students at any age level, and many of them can be used with equal success as group activities or as individual assignments. In addition, the Index of Language Skills indicates which of the four skills (listening, speaking, reading, and writing) are developed and practiced in each activity. With the help of this index, teachers can select activities that will provide needed practice in each of these areas. Thus, the book can be used according to the learning style categories and/or the language skills designations.

For more advanced classes, the author has developed two companion books of activities and blackline masters, *Intermediate Activities for English Language Learners* and *Advanced Activities for English Language Learners.* All three books are designed to facilitate both teaching and learning the English language by providing flexible, ready-to-use supplementary materials.

The Twelve Learning Styles

1. The Field Independent Learner

- likes individual projects
- likes independent discovery
- likes factual information
- likes analytic process
- is unconventional
- sees spatial relationships well
- shows good visual differentiation
- memorizes well
- works well alone
- enjoys puzzles, riddles, and library research

2. The Field Dependent Learner

- likes contact with the teacher
- likes contact with environment and social surrounding
- is group oriented and humorous
- has a good imagination
- accepts external direction
- needs reassurance and teacher modeling
- sees perceptual field as a whole
- enjoys people and group work
- needs teacher praise
- imitates well
- is peer conscious
- enjoys field trips
- prefers explanations first

3. The Cognitive Complexity Learner

- organizes material well
- puts it in relationship to other material
- follows step-by-step directions
- prioritizes and categorizes
- uses vertical analysis of relationships
- is scientific
- likes sequential thinking, dimensions of likeness, reporting, hierarchies, and alphabetizing
- is a good organizer
- enjoys forming lists
- needs memory relationships

4. The Cognitive Simplicity Learner

- tends to use detail well
- pays attention to whole
- uses horizontal analysis
- compares, relates on horizontal dimension
- sees dimension of difference readily
- finds opposites easily
- needs work on similarities
- enjoys grammar, language, and multicultural activities
- likes comparing questions

5. The Convergent Thinker

- uses conventional reasoning
- searches for logical conclusions
- seeks clear-cut answers
- likes decision making
- enjoys scientific activities
- does well on multiple-choice questions
- is good at deduction
- is science oriented
- likes to make judgments
- goes from the general to the particular
- enjoys research

6. The Divergent Thinker

- considers alternative paths
- likes problem solving
- uses imaginative thinking
- makes good decisions
- initiates new ideas
- seeks new approaches
- is artistic and creative
- takes risks
- offers original responses
- thinks of different possible solutions
- enjoys make-believe and role-playing
- will volunteer

The following learning styles are usually characteristic of more mature students.

7. The Analytic Learner

- analyzes details
- pays attention to similarities and differences
- likes independent work
- organizes material well to complete a project
- focuses on facts, dates
- works well with small details
- enjoys description
- enjoys puzzles, building, and map work
- learns dates easily
- likes statistics
- is grammar conscious

8. The Synthesizer

- learns rational concepts easily
- is thematic and descriptive
- sees entire conceptual field
- finds connection between parts
- may miss details
- is impulsive
- learns relational concepts
- has large perceptual field
- puts together parts of a whole
- can find the theme of a story
- needs work on details
- writes well
- enjoys nature

9. The Sharpener

- notices changes
- differentiates new instances from old ones
- creates new categories to hold information
- keeps successive stimulating situations separate
- is scientific
- enjoys research, especially in history and literature
- pays close attention
- adapts well to change
- likes analogies and prioritizing

10. The Leveler

- is often unaware of change
- is often unaware of differences between new and old
- assimilates new stimuli to already dominant cognitive organization
- shows artistic tendencies
- likes to create and try new ideas
- may be a dreamer
- needs work on recognizing differences
- likes many different tasks
- learns the same material from many different methods

11. The Scanner

- is meticulous about detail
- likes deduction and analysis
- sees broad to narrow views
- focuses on details
- tries repeatedly to solve problems
- learns from mistakes, and will try again
- sees details *and* periphery
- puts nothing in secondary position
- tends to be patient
- learns by doing
- enjoys math
- is neat
- can pick out a theme

12. The Focuser

- learns successive items separately
- jumps to conclusions
- creates new categories for information
- notices changes
- has prioritizing skills
- pays little attention to peripheral clues
- relates all available information
- pays attention to a few key details
- needs data-gathering and analytic skills
- needs group work
- tells stories well
- remembers small items
- enjoys art, word problems, and telling stories

Procedure

To make the most effective use of this book, the English language teacher should follow these steps:

1. Observe the students' attitudes, preferences, behaviors, thinking processes, and special difficulties.

2. Decide which learning style(s) most nearly match the needs or dispositions observed.

3. Choose a lesson plan from the category you have selected.

4. Read over the lesson plan and duplicate the accompanying worksheet(s).

5. Proceed according to the plan.

6. Reinforce important concepts through the extension activities suggested.

7. Repeat the activities where necessary and/or create similar materials incorporating ideas from other lessons.

Index of Language Skills

As an additional means of helping teachers select the most effective activities to use with their students, this index shows which of the four language skills *(listening, speaking, reading,* and *writing)* are developed and practiced in each activity.

Lesson Plans

Section 1: The Field Independent Learner

Activity 1

Rationale: This activity requires students to work individually and independently. It involves understanding of spatial relationships and differentiating within a perceptual field. These styles of learning are utilized by the field independent student.

Objective: The students will read and analyze sequential instructions and reinforce their knowledge of prepositions and classroom vocabulary. Prepositions reviewed in this activity are *under, up, across, down, into, around, behind, to,* and *on*.

Materials: Worksheets A and B, scissors, paste; crayons (optional)

Procedure: Pass out copies of the two worksheets. Then have the students cut out the numbered butterflies on Worksheet A and paste them onto the picture of the classroom on Worksheet B. The students must follow the directions on Worksheet A to find out exactly where to paste each butterfly. You may instruct the students to color the butterflies and Worksheet B if you wish.

Extension Activities:

1. After the students have pasted the butterflies onto the picture of the classroom, you could ask, "Butterfly #1, #2, etc., where are you?" The students should answer in complete sentences, based on their pictures.

2. You may ask questions such as, "Butterfly #5, are you in the wastebasket?" The students must look at their pictures and answer, "Yes, I am," or "No, I'm not. I'm on the window."

3. Students could write sentences using the prepositions *into, up, on, down, around, under, to, across,* and *behind*.

4. You could read the following sentences to the class, asking students to draw a picture for each one.

   a. The pencil is on the desk.

   b. The dog is under the chair.

   c. The hat is behind the bed.

   d. The bird is in the tree.

   e. The ribbon is around the package.

   f. The cat fell down the well.

Activity 2

Rationale: This activity is appropriate for field independent learners because they handle individual projects well and are motivated towards self-discovery. The activity is teacher-led and encourages students to discover time relationships in their everyday lives.

Objectives: Students will recreate a day in their lives and account for their activities on that day by conceptualizing those activities onto a diagram. Using the verb "to spend" in relation to time, the students will write and verbalize statements about their diagrams.

Materials: paper and a pencil for each student

Procedure: Tell students to draw a circle on a piece of paper and to label it "My Activity Pie." Then, instruct them to divide the pie into pieces representing the amount of time they spend doing various activities in a typical day. Since it is difficult to account for every hour of any one day, encourage them to diagram their general tendencies.

A finished pie might look like this:

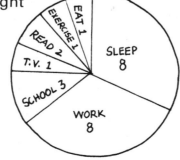

When everyone has completed this task, proceed to the following exercises.

1. Prompt students to talk about their activities using sentences such as:

   I spend two hours working.
   I spend one hour eating.

2. Have students exchange papers and form sentences about their classmates. This provides practice of third person singular verb endings. For example:

   Mary spends four hours exercising.
   Peter spends eight hours sleeping.

3. Model the following patterns for responses:

   I spend more time _____ than _____.

   I spend less time _____ than _____.

4. Have students talk about how they would prefer to spend their time, using the expression "I'd like." For example:

   I spend one hour exercising. I'd like to spend two.
   I spend eight hours working. I'd like to spend six.

5. Ask students to draw an activity pie reflecting a day in the life of a friend or relative. Encourage them to write sentences using the same structures practiced in class.

Activity 3

Rationale: This activity is suitable for field independent learners, since it involves independent work and little contact with the teacher. The level of difficulty of the words used in this exercise can be modified to suit the age, proficiency, and interests of the students.

Objectives: Students will become familiar with the dictionary and how to use it. They will also be introduced to simple adjectives.

Materials: worksheet, dictionaries, and a *Word Box* with adjective cards (see note below)

Procedure: Review the order of the letters in the alphabet. Then introduce the idea of using a dictionary, explaining what it is, why we have them, and how they are used. Allow each student to hold a dictionary and page through it. Show students how to locate words that begin with a particular letter. Distribute the worksheets to the students, and have them find words that begin with the six letters they are given. When they have found a word for each letter, have them select six cards from the *Word Box* and use each pair of words in a short sentence.

Note: You can make a *Word Box* by filling any small box with cards on which you have written different words (one word per card). For this activity, every card should have an adjective on it.

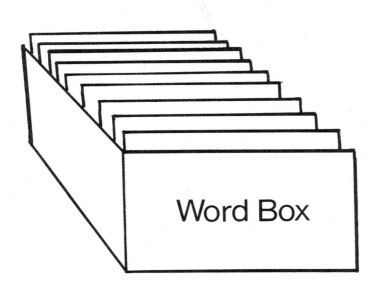

Word Box

Section 2: The Field Dependent Learner

Activity 4

Rationale: This lesson involves teacher contact, is group oriented, and calls for external direction. The students' responses are checked and reinforced frequently. These styles of learning are characteristic of the field dependent student.

Objectives: The students will learn various shapes (line, circle, square, triangle, and rectangle) through the use of the prepositions *in, on,* and *under.*

Materials: Worksheets A and B

Procedure: Pass out copies of Worksheet A and read the following directions to the class. Check the students' papers as they work, or collect them when everyone is done.

1. Draw an X *in* the triangle.

2. Write your name *on* the line.

3. Draw a cat *in* the rectangle.

4. Draw a dog *under* the square.

5. Draw a face *in* the circle.

Extension Activities:

1. Use Worksheet B to further practice listening comprehension and reinforce the prepositions *in, on,* and *under.* The words *house, roof,* and *chimney* will also be reviewed. Pass out the second worksheet, and direct students to

   a. Draw a bird *on* the chimney.
   b. Draw a girl *in* the house.
   c. Draw a dog *under* the house.

2. Both worksheets can be used to practice other directions, including *next to, over, above, beside, to the right, to the left,* etc.

3. After the students have followed your directions, have them tell you where each item is on their worksheets; for example, *The face is in the circle* or *The bird is on the chimney.*

4. Have the students take turns asking each other where different items on their worksheets are.

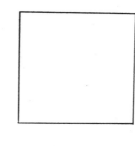
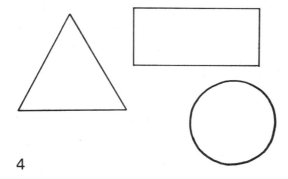

Activity 5

Rationale: This activity is appropriate for field dependent students since it involves guidance and demonstration from the teacher, and encourages students to seek teacher approval.

Objectives: The students will recognize words that begin with the same consonant sound, and will be able to use question words, i.e., *who, what, when, where, why,* and *how.*

Materials: worksheet and example page (see Procedure)

Procedure: Before class, prepare an example page by pasting pictures of three different objects on one piece of paper. Two of the three objects pictured should start with the same consonant sound.

In class, hold up your example page and model the desired consonant sound. Then say the name of each object clearly. Ask students to tell you which two words begin with that sound. When you are sure that all the students understand how to do the activity, hand out a worksheet to each student. Say the name of each object pictured in group one, then tell the students to circle the two pictures that begin with the same sound. Continue in the same manner for the other groups of pictures on the worksheet.

After you have finished this part of the activity, ask the students to write questions about the uncircled object in each group using the question words *who, what, when, where, why,* and *how.* (For example: *What is that?, Where do we find it?, Why do we use it?)*

Activity 6

Rationale: This activity is suitable for field dependent learners because they are socially oriented and do not like to work alone. They prefer activities in which the teacher provides models and assurances.

Objectives: Students will improve their speaking and listening skills and review the names of foods.

Materials: worksheet, foods for making salad (lettuce, cucumbers, etc.), price tags, money

Procedure: Before class, obtain money (either real or play) and foods for making salad. Prepare a price tag for each item, then set up a small food shop in your classroom. Divide the class into small groups, and assign one group to be clerks. Pass out copies of the worksheet, and instruct each group to decide what ingredients they will put in their salad.

Have each group make up a shopping list like the one on the worksheet. Next, instruct students on how to shop for the items on their list, and demonstrate for them by purchasing one item yourself. Ask each group to make a trip to the store. Every member of the group should buy at least two items. After each group has been to the store, have the group members tell what they have bought and how they are going to make their salad.

Activity 7

Rationale: Field dependent students need constant reassurance, and tend to give a great deal of attention to persons and things in their social surroundings. This material is well suited for field dependent students because it focuses on the student's home, thereby emphasizing perception awareness.

Objectives: The students will draw plans of their houses or apartments. They will practice speaking skills and review adjectives by describing their homes to the class, listing colors, items, and relative positions of trees, bushes, sidewalk, etc.

Materials: worksheet, paper, colored pencils or crayons

Procedure: Pass out paper and colored pencils or crayons. Have each student make a detailed sketch of his or her home, including rooms, furniture, and outside foliage (if any). Next, distribute the worksheets and review the list of adjectives. Have each student choose one room from his or her home and describe it using as many adjectives as possible from the list. The students can be divided into small groups to ask each other the questions on the worksheet. Lastly, the students can explain the layout of one room and tell why they like it.

Section 3: The Cognitive Complexity Learner

Activity 8

Rationale: This exercise is appropriate for the cognitive complexity student because it uses vertical analysis, has step-by-step instructions, and uses simple categorizing.

Objectives: Students will learn basic sentence structures and practice writing sentences. (Students must already know the conjugation of the verb *to be* and *-ing* forms.)

Materials: worksheet, pencils

Procedure: If necessary, review the conjugations of *to be* and the formation of *-ing* words. Then pass out the worksheets and instruct students to fill in the answers, using the pictures at the bottom of the worksheet as clues.

Extension Activities: Ask questions, based on the pictures, that will elicit negative answers. For example:

Is Joe swimming?

Are they thinking?

Am I crying?

Ask *what* questions based on the pictures:

What is Sam doing?

What is Joe doing?

What am I doing?

You could also ask questions about what various students in the class are doing. Other verbs, such as *laughing, talking, playing, singing, dancing, looking,* etc., could be used and acted out by the students.

Activity 9

Rationale: This material is well suited to cognitive complexity learners, for they are skilled in prioritizing, sequential thinking, and giving step-by-step instructions.

Objectives: Students will practice speaking and learn new vocabulary.

Materials: Worksheets A, B, and C; cardboard

Procedure: Before class, copy the worksheets, glue them onto cardboard, and cut them apart to form a set of twenty-one activity cards. (If you have more than twenty-one students in your class, you may want to make up some extra cards.) Place the cards face down in a box, or hold them like playing cards, with the blank side of the cards facing the students. Have each student draw a card from your set, and allow the students time to reflect upon the steps involved in their activities. Encourage them to jot down ideas. Finally, have each student describe the steps involved in his or her activity to the class.

Example:

Making a
sandwich

First, I will get some bread. Then I will find some peanut butter and some jelly. Next, I will put some peanut butter on the bread with a knife. Then I will . . .

Activity 10

Rationale: This activity is appropriate for the cognitive complexity learner because it involves the organization of items into alphabetical order.

Objective: Students will alphabetize the items pictured on the worksheet.

Materials: worksheet, pencils

Procedure: Review the order of the letters in the alphabet and distribute the worksheets. Identify the objects pictured on the worksheet. Then instruct students to write the names of the objects in alphabetical order.

Extension Activities: Make a picture dictionary with the students, having them draw or cut out magazine pictures of objects that start with each letter. As a variation, ask them to use objects that fall under a particular category, such as "animals" or "clothing."

Just for Fun: Have a contest! Give the students five words, and see who can put them in order first.

Activity 11

Rationale: This activity is appropriate for cognitive complexity learners, since they tend to solve problems step by step. They also perform well on analyzing relationships vertically.

Objectives: Using Total Physical Response (TPR) techniques, students will improve their listening ability, review imperative sentences, and practice sequential concepts.

Materials: a series of commands like those provided below

Procedure: Divide the students into groups. (The number of students in each group will depend on your class size and the amount of time available for the activity.) Line up the members of each group as for a relay race. Tell the students that you will give a series of commands. The person at the front of each line is to follow the first command as quickly as possible.

Give the first command, and award one point to the student who completes the action most quickly and correctly.

The person at the front of each line should then move to the back, and the next student in each group follows your next command. Continue in this manner, using the sample commands below and any others you wish to add.

Keep a running total of the number of points awarded to members of each team. At the end of the game, declare one team the winner!

Sample commands:

1. Before you stand up, tell me your name.

2. Draw a flower first, then go shut the door.

3. After you pick up my book, read a line to me.

4. Do three things: first, close your eyes; second, raise your hands; and third, open your mouth.

5. Walk to the front of the room, then run to the back.

6. Before you jump to your left, move forward two steps.

7. Write my name on the board after you touch my hands.

8. First show me your homework, then answer the question.

Activity 12

Rationale: This activity allows the cognitive complexity student to use his or her organizational skills and facility with vertical analysis.

Objective: The students will learn common cooking terms, focusing on verbs and units of measure.

Materials: worksheet, pencils

Procedure: Pass out a copy of the worksheet to each student. Review any cooking terms the students already know, and introduce those that are new. Ask students to put the directions for making brownies in correct step-by-step order, writing the appropriate number in the blank before each step. Ask students to change the measurements to the metric system, using the table provided. Discuss the students' favorite foods and ask each student to briefly describe how his or her favorite food is prepared.

Extension Activity: If you have the necessary time and facilities, bring the ingredients to class and make brownies together.

Section 4: The Cognitive Simplicity Learner

Activity 13

Rationale: This activity is appropriate for the cognitive simplicity learner because it involves comparing and relating items on a horizontal dimension.

Objectives: Students will practice the alphabet, using capital letters, after the teacher reviews the letters. The class will discuss Halloween customs.

Materials: worksheet; crayons (optional)

Procedure: Instruct students to fill in the missing letters on the worksheet. Remind them to use capital letters.

Extension Activity: Students can color the leaves on the worksheet following your instructions, e.g., "Color leaf A yellow."

Activity 14

Rationale: The cognitive simplicity learner compares and relates in a horizontal fashion. This activity makes use of that skill by requiring students to find similarities and differences between words presented on a string chart.

Objectives: Students will practice vowel sounds and be able to find the one word that doesn't fit in a series.

Materials: a string chart, eight packets containing four words each, one packet of ten words to be displayed on the teacher's desk

Procedure: Before class, make a string chart and the necessary packets of words. A string chart is a long piece of string hung horizontally and fastened at either end to the wall or blackboard. Slips of paper containing the structure to be practiced are folded and hung on the string. The words to be printed on each slip of paper appear on the next page.

Take one of the eight packets of four words, and place one word from that packet on the string chart. (It may help to underline the target sound in red.) Ask each student to pronounce the word, then hang the rest of the words from that packet on the string chart. One of the words will not contain the target sound. Ask a student to take off the word that doesn't go with the others, then replace it with a word from the packet of ten words that should be laid out on your desk or a table. Model the pronunciation of all the words on the chart, having the class repeat after you. Take off the words from that packet, and continue with the next vowel sound to be practiced, using the next packet of words in the same manner.

Words to be used in the eight packets:

Packet 1 (vowel sound: $[ɑy]$)

k<u>i</u>nd   line   since   buy

Packet 2 (vowel sound: $[ə]$)

f<u>u</u>n   young   tune   money

Packet 3 (vowel sound: $[ɛ]$)

g<u>e</u>t   egg   bread   eight

Packet 4 (vowel sound: $[ʊ]$)

b<u>oo</u>k   cool   could   full

Packet 5 (vowel sound: $[uw]$)

f<u>oo</u>l   who   blue   good

Packet 6 (vowel sound: $[ɪ]$)

sw<u>i</u>m   mitten   ship   find

Packet 7 (vowel sound: $[i]$)

m<u>e</u>   three   fit   easy

Packet 8 (vowel sound: $[ɑw]$)

h<u>ou</u>se   down   phone   our

Words to lay out on your desk:

climb	some	sled	hood	winter
east	flower	fall	cat	snow

Activity 15

Rationale: This activity is well suited for cognitive simplicity learners, for it encourages the use of detail while paying attention to the whole, thus allowing the student to find similarities and differences.

Objectives: Students will compare and contrast the fruits and vegetables pictured on the worksheet, noting the similarities and differences between them.

Materials: worksheet; crayons (optional)

Procedure: Pass out copies of the worksheet, and instruct the students to note the similarities and differences between the objects in the picture; e.g., which is a fruit and which is a vegetable, which are round, etc. The students can determine whether or not all fruits are round or all vegetables are round. They can also compare and contrast the fruits and vegetables by color. Students can determine whether or not all fruits grow on vines or beneath the ground.

Extension Activity: Bring in various fruits and vegetables for further comparisons, such as soft and hard.

Activity 16

Rationale: This activity exercises the cognitive simplicity learner's inclination to use detail and see whole pictures (attention to the whole).

Objectives: The students will practice speaking and use new vocabulary.

Materials: Worksheets A, B, and C; cardboard

Procedure: Before class, copy the worksheets, glue them onto cardboard, and cut them apart to form a set of twenty-one scene cards. (If you have more than twenty-one students in your class, you may want to make up some extra scene cards.) Place the cards face down in a box, or hold them like playing cards, with the blank side of the cards facing the students. Have each student draw a card, and allow the students time to reflect upon the scenes they have chosen. Encourage them to jot down details of those scenes. Finally, have each student describe his or her scene to the class, using as much detail as possible.

Example:

A bakery store window

I see a white wedding cake.

Behind the cake are chocolate eclairs.

There are many cherry tarts.

An apple pie is . . .

16

Activity 17

Rationale: This activity is appropriate for cognitive simplicity learners, since they tend to compare and relate things on a horizontal dimension.

Objectives: Students will review words already learned and improve their spelling skills by comparing and relating.

Materials: worksheet, or blackboard and chalk

Procedure: This activity may be done in one of two ways:

1. Distribute copies of the worksheet. Review the concept of analogies, and make sure that the students are familiar with the vocabulary on the worksheet. Have the students fill in the blanks in the analogy chart.

2. Copy the analogy chart at each end of the blackboard, and divide the class into two groups. Line up each group in front of one of the charts. In the form of a relay race, have the students take turns going to the board and filling in blanks in the analogy chart. (Each student should fill in only one blank per turn.) The group that fills out the chart most quickly and correctly wins the game.

Note: Other analogy charts could be created using words learned in previous class lessons, then used in one of the above ways.

Section 5: The Convergent Thinker

Activity 18

Rationale: This activity appeals to the convergent thinker's ability to succeed on multiple-choice tests. It also employs conventional reasoning and clear-cut answers.

Objective: The students will review and demonstrate their knowledge of the parts of the body.

Materials: worksheet, pencils

Procedure: Lead the class in a quick game of "Simon Says" as an oral review of body parts. Pass out copies of the worksheet and instruct the class to fill in the blanks with the correct answers. Remind them that this is not a test, but a review.

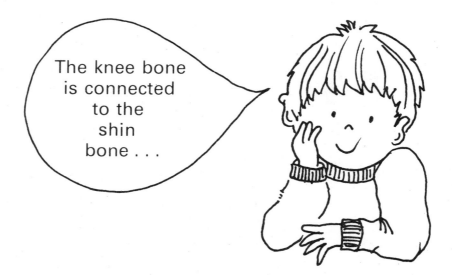

The knee bone is connected to the shin bone . . .

Activity 19

Rationale: Convergent thinkers use conventional reasoning to reach logical conclusions. This activity is appropriate for convergent thinkers, because they do well on scientific activities and problems with clear-cut answers.

Objective: Students will learn to distinguish between voiced and voiceless sounds.

Materials: worksheet, pencils

Procedure: Explain and demonstrate to the students that when you pronounce a voiced consonant, you can feel the vibration of your vocal cords if you put your fingers on your throat. Voiceless consonants do not produce this vibration. Pass out copies of the worksheet, and ask the students to use the method described above to determine which words start with voiced or voiceless consonants. The students should write each word under the correct category (voiced or voiceless) on the worksheet. Finally, have the students write down three more words for each category.

Extension Activity: You could make up different word lists to reinforce and provide further practice of voiced and voiceless consonants.

Activity 20

Rationale: This activity utilizes conventional reasoning and logic. Clear-cut answers make the activity especially appropriate for the convergent thinker.

Objectives: The students will enrich their general vocabulary and learn the names of different types of stores.

Materials: worksheet, pictures of a variety of objects (at least five per student), blank index cards (3 x 5 or 4 x 6 size, pictures must fit on cards), markers or crayons, glue

Procedure: Pass out copies of the worksheet. Ask the students to draw a line from each object to the store in which that object could be found. Then have the students name one other object which can be found in each of the stores listed on the worksheet. (You may ask them to do this orally or by writing the name of the object next to the appropriate store on the worksheet.)

Next, give each student a set of five (or more) pictures of different objects. (You may either provide these pictures yourself, or ask the students to bring them to class as a homework assignment.) Have the students paste their pictures onto individual cards. Then, ask them to write the name of the place where each object can be found on a different card. Each student should end up with a set of five picture cards and a set of five word cards.

Divide the students into pairs, and have them exchange their cards with their partners. The partners should then test each other, saying the name of each object pictured and the name of the place where it can be found.

Section 6: The Divergent Thinker

Activity 21

Rationale: This activity is well suited for divergent thinkers, because they consider alternative possibilities. They also tend to be creative and field-independent.

Objectives: The students will improve their writing, speaking, and listening skills, and practice making simple sentences.

Materials: worksheet, paper, pencils; crayons (optional)

Procedure: Pass out copies of the worksheet, and discuss the picture of the future world. Next, ask the students to use their imagination and draw their own pictures of the future world. After they have finished their pictures, have the students write descriptions of the future worlds they have drawn, using simple sentences. (See the example sentences on the worksheet.) Display the students' drawings, and let the students discuss the future worlds they have drawn.

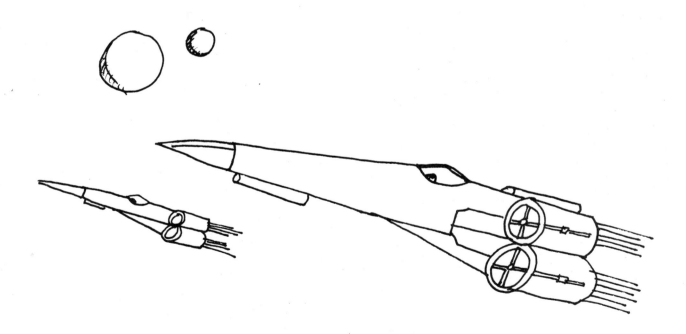

Activity 22

Rationale: This activity is appropriate for divergent thinkers, since it gives students the opportunity to be imaginative and artistic.

Objectives: The students will draw the human body, and use the appropriate vocabulary words to label it.

Materials: worksheet, pencils

Procedure: Pass out copies of the worksheet, and review the parts of the body by playing "Simon Says." Ask the students to draw a human body and label each part with the correct word from the vocabulary list.

Activity 23

Rationale: This activity allows divergent thinkers to use their problem-solving abilities and to capitalize on their imaginative talents.

Objectives: Students will review prepositions and vegetable names. This activity should also initiate a discussion about gardening, cooking, or eating vegetables.

Materials: worksheet, pencils, crayons or colored pencils

Procedure: Distribute a copy of the worksheet to each student. Review the names of the vegetables listed on the worksheet through a short discussion of students' preferences: "I like _____," "I don't like _____," etc. Then ask the students to color each vegetable picture on the worksheet, and to label each picture with the correct word from the vocabulary list. Next, review the prepositions listed on the worksheet, and have the students fill in the blanks in the sentences at the bottom of the worksheet. Correct the sentences as a class. Finally, ask the students to write five more sentences using the names of the vegetables and the prepositions listed on the worksheet.

Note: In order to label the pictures and fill in the blanks, the students will need to be familiar with the plural forms of the vegetable names listed on the worksheet.

Extension Activities: You could ask the students to draw a picture of a garden on a separate piece of paper, then cut out the vegetable pictures from the worksheet and paste them onto the garden. Also, you could introduce the terms *cooked* and *raw,* and ask the students to tell how each vegetable can be eaten.

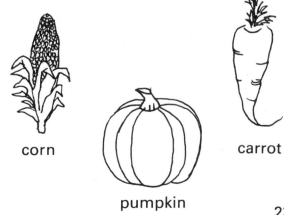

pepper

tomato

corn

pumpkin

carrot

lettuce

Activity 24

Rationale: This activity is appropriate for divergent thinkers because it encourages the generation of alternative possibilities and involves imaginative and creative thinking.

Objectives: This activity will enrich the students' vocabulary and their understanding of English, and motivate them to produce their new language.

Materials: worksheet, pencils

Procedure: Discuss the topic of "home life" with the students in general terms. Explain that many different types of people call on us at our homes, some of whom we welcome and others whom we would rather not see. Next, distribute copies of the worksheet. Be sure the students understand the three situations pictured, then have them write what they would say in each situation.

Extension Activity: Ask the students who else they can think of that might come to their door. What would they say to each of those people? Divide the students into pairs, and have each pair make up a dialogue with one of the persons listed below (or any other persons generated in your discussion). Finally, have each pair role-play its conversation for the class.

1. a bill collector

2. a talkative neighbor

3. a plumber

4. someone collecting money for a charity

Activity 25

Rationale: This activity provides divergent thinkers with the opportunity to consider alternative possibilities for problem solving and to think imaginatively and creatively.

Objectives: Students will review vocabulary while learning about the origins of Thanksgiving, and the manner in which it is celebrated in the United States.

Materials: worksheet, pencils

Procedure: This activity works well as a vocabulary review to follow up an in-class discussion of Thanksgiving customs. Distribute copies of the worksheet and have the students do the crossword puzzle individually. When everyone is finished, correct as a class.

Answers:

Section 7: The Analytic Learner

Activity 26

Rationale: This activity requires students to analyze visual details and focus on facts, details, and description. These styles of learning are characteristic of the analytic learner.

Objective: The students will review family vocabulary.

Materials: Worksheets A, B, C, D, and E; pencils

Procedure: Pass out copies of Worksheet A, and discuss the family pictured on it. Be sure all students are familiar with the relationship words *father, mother, sister, brother, son, daughter, grandfather, grandmother, grandson, granddaughter, husband,* and *wife.* (These words are listed on Worksheet D). Then distribute copies of Worksheets B, C, and D. Go over the example exercise on Worksheet B as a class, then have the students complete the exercises on all three worksheets individually.

Extension Activity: Pass out copies of Worksheet E, and have the students draw pictures of the members of their families.

JOAQUIN   ANA

ENRIQUE

CARMELA

Activity 27

Rationale: This activity is well suited for analytic learners, because it requires students to be attentive to similarities and differences. Students must also focus on details and words to organize and complete the task.

Objectives: In this activity, students will gain skill in classifying words, utilize their knowledge of vocabulary, and use discrimination in choosing the best answers.

Materials: worksheet, pencils, paper

Procedure: Pass out copies of the worksheet, and have the students read the list of vocabulary words. Then have the students categorize the words by writing each word under the appropriate picture. Finally, ask the students to write a short paragraph about each of the three buildings, using the vocabulary words listed below it.

Section 8: The Synthesizer

Activity 28

Rationale: In this activity the student is encouraged to see parts of a whole. This ability is characteristic of the synthesizer.

Objective: Students will learn the names of animals and their babies.

Materials: worksheet, scissors, paste, pencils

Procedure: Teach or review the names of the following animals and their babies: *dog/puppy, horse/colt, cat/kitten,* and *pig/piglet.* Then pass out copies of the worksheet. Instruct the students to draw a line from each mother animal to her baby. Next, have the students cut out the names of the animals from the bottom of the worksheet and paste them under the correct pictures.

Activity 29

Rationale: The synthesizer learns by rationalizing concepts. This activity is appropriate for the synthesizer because it introduces occupations by means of conceptual drawings.

Objectives: Students will learn about different occupations and will be able to associate thematic vocabulary and activities with appropriate occupations.

Materials: Worksheets A, B, and C; pencils

Procedure: Pass out copies of Worksheets A and B, and ask your students to guess what occupation is depicted in each picture. Discuss the vocabulary items found in each picture and their relationship to the occupation. Next, hand out Worksheet C and have students complete the exercise in class.

Extension Activities:

1. For a quick drill on a subsequent day, give a one-word cue and have the students supply the occupation that relates to the cue.

Example:

Teacher: type

Student: secretary

Teacher: hospital

Student: doctor

2. After the students are very familiar with the twelve occupations in this activity, discuss other occupations and associated vocabulary and activities.

Activity 30

Rationale: This activity capitalizes on the synthesizer's ability to make connections between parts, and further develops his or her talent for working thematically and descriptively.

Objective: Students will review the conjugations of irregular verbs, then write a short story in the simple past. This activity will stimulate vocabulary skills, while strengthening the synthesizer's work with detail.

Materials: Worksheets A and B, pencils

Procedure: Hand out copies of Worksheets A and B, and review any difficult vocabulary words. Ask the students to find the past tense of each verb listed, and to write the correct forms in the blanks provided. Correct in class.

Next, direct students' attention to the bottom half of Worksheet B, and ask them to identify the verbs with only the pictures to guide them. They must write the infinitive form and the past tense in the blanks provided. Correct as a class.

Finally, have each student write a brief story using at least five of the sentence fragments (subject and verb pairs) given. You may want to suggest a theme. After they have been corrected, read several stories to the class and use them as the basis for class discussion.

Activity 31

Rationale: This activity is well suited for synthesizers, because they enjoy music, are descriptive, and see conceptual fields in their entirety.

Objective: Students will use their English writing skills in a stimulating setting.

Materials: any classical record or cassette tape, worksheet, paper, and pencils

Procedure: Distribute copies of the worksheet, and ask the students either to describe the scene they see or to write a story about it. Turn on the classical music while the students are writing.

Note: This activity can also be done using magazine pictures or posters of nature scenes in place of the worksheet.

Section 9: The Sharpener

Activity 32

Rationale: This activity is appropriate for the sharpener because it involves differentiating between items and noticing differences.

Objective: Students will identify and label pictures of opposites, then write statements describing the pictures.

Materials: worksheet, paper, and pencils

Procedure: Pass out copies of the worksheet, and review the opposites listed on it. Identify the pictures together, and instruct the students to label the pictures with words from the list. Next, use the examples below as you instruct the students to write statements describing the pictures. It may be necessary for you to supply the students with verbs and names of objects in the pictures.

Example:
   1A. The roots are deep.
   1B. The roots are shallow.

Extension Activity: You could ask the students to write a statement using the present progressive tense to describe each picture.

Activity 33

Rationale: This activity is appropriate for sharpeners, because it encourages them to notice changes and differences.

Objectives: Students will gain understanding of classmates who come from different backgrounds, and learn about the different ethnic groups within the United States. They will practice their speaking and writing skills without constant supervision.

Materials: worksheet, pencils

Procedure: Explain to the students that many different cultures are represented in the classroom, and that they are going to learn about these cultures. Divide the class into pairs and give one copy of the worksheet to each pair. Have the students ask their partners the questions in the diagram, and write their answers in the spaces provided. After the students have completed the entire exercise, have them introduce each other to the class until all of the students have had a chance to speak.

Activity 34

Rationale: This material is suitable for sharpeners, because it requires students to organize material into categories and notice changes.

Objectives: The students will learn the months of the year, the seasons, and which months fall within each season.

Materials: worksheet, scissors

Procedure: Pass out copies of the worksheet. Have the students cut out the rectangles and mix them up. Then have the students place the months in order beginning with January. Next, discuss the four seasons, and ask the students to place the months under the seasons in which they belong. As a variation, have the students place the months in alphabetical order.

Examples:

Alphabetical:

April	January	May
August	July	November
December	June	October
February	March	September

Under seasons:

Spring	*Summer*
March	June
April	July
May	August

Fall	*Winter*
September	December
October	January
November	February

Extension Activities:

1. The class could discuss various holidays and decide in which season each one falls.

2. The students could categorize their birthdays by season and/or month.

Activity 35

Rationale: This activity makes use of a sharpener's ability to notice changes.

Objective: Students will have the opportunity to learn new vocabulary in a game-like activity.

Materials: worksheet, and some, half, or all of the following household items:

1. battery
2. thermometer
3. candle
4. glass jar
5. sponge
6. bell
7. mirror
8. screwdriver
9. thimble
10. hammer
11. shoehorn
12. mousetrap
13. golf tee
14. ice pick
15. paintbrush
16. deck of cards
17. cotton balls
18. Band-Aid
19. toothbrush
20. flashlight
21. salt shaker
22. nutcracker
23. pot holder
24. candle snuffer
25. bottle of vitamins

Procedure: Before the students come to class, hide the items around the room so that they are subtly visible. Meet each student at the door of the classroom, and hand him or her a copy of the worksheet. Have the students work silently and individually as they hunt for the hidden items. Instruct them to sit down and fill in the use of each item on the worksheet after they have found all 25. This activity may be a contest to see who can find all the hidden items first. When your students are seated and have completed their hunt sheets to the best of their ability, discuss the items and their functions.

Note: Be sure to instruct the students to leave each object in its hiding place. They are to write down the name of an object when they find it, rather than taking it.

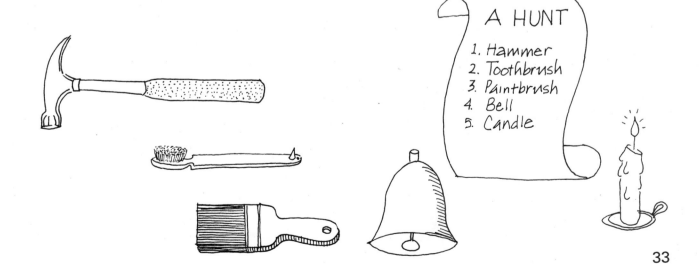

Section 10: The Leveler

Activity 36

Rationale: This activity is appropriate for levelers since it is based on a topic to which all students can relate equally.

Objectives: Students will learn the names of the parts of the body, and understand the importance of good health.

Materials: worksheet, pencils; picture cards showing parts of the body (optional)

Procedure: Use a dual approach to facilitate learning as you introduce the names of the body parts—for example, show a picture card of a body part and say its name simultaneously. Drill the students to test their ability to recall the new vocabulary. Next, pass out copies of the worksheet, and ask the students to identify the body parts shown.

Extension Activities: Give the students a short lecture on the importance of a well-balanced diet. Discuss the four basic food groups: meats, dairy products, vegetables, and bread or cereal. Ask the students to plan nutritious meals for one day.

Activity 37

Rationale: This activity is appropriate for the leveler, because it involves assimilating new stimuli into already dominant cognitive organizations.

Objective: Students will reinforce their knowledge of the present progressive tense by writing sentences using the subjects listed A-M on the worksheet.

Materials: worksheet, pencils

Procedure: Distribute copies of the worksheet, and review the present progressive verbs that are pictured in the boxes. Practice using the verbs in sentences: e.g., *The girl is jumping.* Read the subjects listed A-M with the students, and instruct the students to complete each sentence using the verb indicated by the number. Do A together as an example. (**Note:** It may be necessary to practice statements that use *are* instead of *is.)*

Activity 38

Rationale: A leveler generalizes and categorizes new material. In this activity, students will collect responses to a question, and make generalizations based on those responses.

Objective: The students will practice using *everyone, most, some,* and *no one* to categorize responses to questions.

Materials: worksheet, paper, pencils

Procedure: Pass out copies of the worksheet, and review (or introduce) each structure using the illustrations. Then have each student choose a question from the bottom half of the worksheet, or assign one question to each student. Tell them to walk around the room, asking their question to each one of their classmates, and recording the number of positive and negative responses. Stress that the questions require a *yes* or *no* answer only. When the students have completed their inquiries, have them report the results to the class, using one of the new structures (*everyone, most, some,* or *no one*).

Activity 39

Rationale: This material is suitable for the leveler because it assimilates new stimuli to already dominant cognitive organizations.

Objective: The students will create questions and statements using only the words provided. (The students must already know the words given in order to create new sentences.)

Materials: worksheet, scissors

Procedure: Distribute copies of the worksheet. Have the students cut out the rectangles and mix them up. Then have the students arrange the words to make as many questions and statements as they can. You may ask the students to work alone, in small groups, or as a class.

Example sentences:

Where are you going?

I am going fishing.

When are you going?

When is he going?

Is he going running?

What is he doing?

Is he fishing?

Are you running?

What is your name?

Is your name _____?

Are you _____?

Who are you? Who is he?

Who is going fishing?

Where is he going fishing?

Where are you going running?

Section 11: The Scanner

Activity 40

Rationale: This activity is appropriate for scanners, because they focus on and are meticulous about detail. Scanners are also good at analysis and deduction.

Objective: Students will learn the reading skills needed to fill out simple forms.

Materials: worksheet, pencils

Procedure: Distribute copies of the worksheet, and ask the students to complete as much of each form as they can. Discuss each form, blank by blank, after the students have attempted to fill out the forms on their own. Using a sample form drawn on the chalkboard, show students how to fill in each form.

Extension Activity: Complete the forms orally.

Activity 41

Rationale: This activity allows the scanner to use his or her ability to work well with detail and deduction.

Objectives: The students will review modes of transportation and compose simple sentences.

Materials: worksheet, paper, pencils

Procedure: Distribute copies of the worksheet, and ask the students to identify each mode of transportation pictured on it. Then, ask the students which mode of transportation would be appropriate for getting to various places, such as school, church, New York City, Paris, the grocery store, a friend or relative's house, etc. Have the students write sentences about how Juanita and Pedro can get to various places using these modes of transportation. Correct the sentences as a class. Finally, have the students write sentences about themselves and the kinds of transportation they normally use, for example: *I ride my bicycle to school.*

Activity 42

Rationale: This activity is appropriate for the scanner, since it involves attention to detail, analysis, and deduction.

Objective: The students will work with one of the most common language functions, apologizing, and enhance their understanding of how to apologize in a variety of situations.

Materials: worksheet, pencils

Procedure: Introduce the concept of apologizing by role-playing one or more simple scenes; e.g., bumping into someone and explaining that you are sorry. Review any necessary phrases and vocabulary. Then, give each student a copy of the worksheet, and ask the students to match each picture with the appropriate apology.

Extension Activities: Role-play the following scenes. Encourage the students to be as enthusiastic as they wish.

1. You are late for an appointment. Apologize and explain why you are late.

2. You want to interrupt someone who is busy.

3. You don't understand someone who is speaking to you. Apologize and request that he or she repeat the statement.

Section 12: The Focuser

Activity 43

Rationale: This activity is well suited for focusers, because they prioritize and compare the available information. Focusers also pay attention to key details and jump to conclusions.

Objectives: The students will read a short paragraph and answer questions about it. They will also write a conclusion for the story.

Materials: Worksheets A, B, and C; pencils

Procedure: Hand out copies of Worksheets A and B. Have the students read the story on Worksheet A silently, then look at the pictures on Worksheet B.

When you are sure that everyone understands the story, distribute copies of Worksheet C. Have the students answer the questions and write a conclusion to the story. Finally, discuss the story and students' conclusions as a class.

Activity 44

Rationale: This activity capitalizes on the focuser's comparing skills and ability to notice changes.

Objective: The students will identify and use simple comparatives and superlatives.

Materials: worksheet, construction paper, glue, scissors, pencils or colored pencils

Procedure: Introduce the following adjectives: *fast, small, tall, big,* and *fat.* Write these words on the blackboard so that students can refer to them throughout this activity. Then review the procedure for forming comparatives and superlatives (adding *-er* or *-est* to single-syllable adjectives). Distribute copies of the worksheet. Ask the students to cut out the pictures, and to arrange them in order to show a comparison between similar objects (e.g., big, bigger, biggest). Have the students label each picture, using the adjectives and their comparative and superlative forms. Ask the students to glue their pictures onto construction paper in the correct order. Students will now have their own "posters."

Activity 45

Rationale: This activity is appropriate for focusers, because they relate all available information to their problem-solving activities, and tend to focus on important details.

Objectives: The students will gain listening and speaking skills that will enable them to perform successfully in job interviews.

Material: worksheet

Procedure: Distribute copies of the worksheet. As a class, read and rehearse the interview. Ask different students to respond to the questions on the interview sheet. Next, switch roles and have the students take turns asking you the interview questions. Be sure to give a variety of answers, so students will have the opportunity to hear appropriate applicant responses.

Discuss and explain the interview format, making a point of discussing interview etiquette. Finally, have the students put away the worksheet. Then role-play sections of an interview with each student individually, as the rest of the class observes.

Extension Activity: Have students practice interviewing one another.

Activity 46

Rationale: This activity is suitable for focusers, because it makes use of their ability to prioritize and compare, to relate all available information, and to create new categories to hold information.

Objectives: The students will learn the names of a variety of fruits, as well as how and when they are grown.

Materials: worksheet, pencils; pictures of a variety of fruits (optional)

Procedure: Discuss a variety of fruits with your class, including when and how they are grown. Be sure to discuss the fruits listed on the worksheet; in addition, you may wish to talk about others. Review the name of each type of fruit, and show pictures to assure comprehension. Next, hand out copies of the worksheet, and ask the students to label each picture with a word from the list. Finally, have the students answer the questions on the worksheet and then discuss their answers in class.

Extension Activities:

1. Make up additional worksheets using different types of fruit.

2. Ask additional questions which require students to look up information in an encyclopedia. Then discuss the answers in class.

3. Have each student prepare an oral report on a different type of fruit, bringing in a sample of the fruit, if it is available.

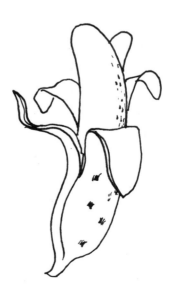

Worksheets

Directions:

Cut out the numbered butterflies and paste them on the picture of the class-room. Follow these directions:

1. Butterfly #1, fly into the room.
2. Butterfly #2, fly across the window.
3. Butterfly #3, fly up to the ceiling.
4. Butterfly #4, fly to the wall.
5. Butterfly #5, fly down to the floor.
6. Butterfly #6, fly into the waste-basket.
7. Butterfly #7, sit on the blackboard.
8. Butterfly #8, fly around the plant.
9. Butterfly #9, fly under the desk.
10. Butterfly #10, fly behind the desk.

Directions:

Find a word in the dictionary that begins with each of the following letters:

B   **G**   **L**

_____   _____   _____

N   **R**   **W**

_____   _____   _____

Use each word in a short sentence or phrase.

1. _____

2. _____

3. _____

4. _____

5. _____

6. _____

Name _____ Date _____ Activity 4-A

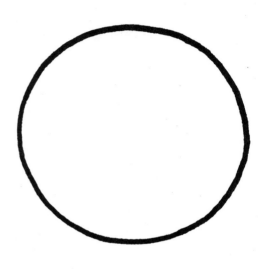
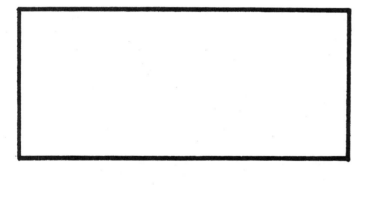
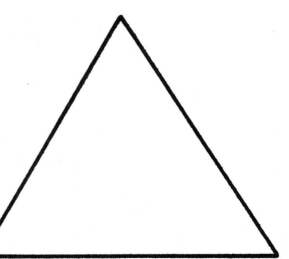

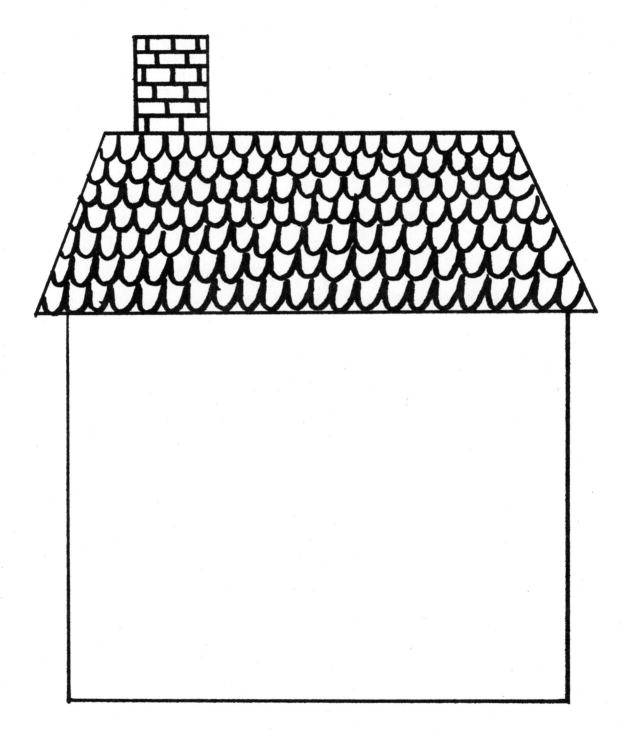

Directions:

With the other members of your group, discuss the ingredients you would like to put in a salad. Make up a shopping list, using the sample list below if you need help. Then go to the store and buy all the items on your list. Each person should take charge of buying at least two items.

Sample shopping list:

a half pound of green peppers

a half pound of onions

two tomatoes

one bottle of salad dressing

one cucumber

one head of lettuce

one pound of carrots

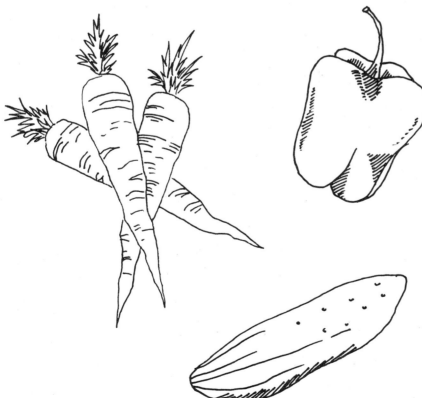

Questions

Where do you live?

What color is your home?

What room does your family use the most?

Are there flowers in your home?

What kinds of books do you have?

In what room is the T.V.?

Do you have any pets?

If yes, where do they sleep?

Which room do you like the best?

What color is this room?

What kind of furniture is in this room?

Adjectives

bright	big	wooden
light	small	fake
dark	large	real
wide	heavy	covered
narrow	light	square
long	pretty	long
high	beautiful	short
soft	unusual ·	ugly
hard	lovely	low

Directions:
Fill in the blanks with the correct verb forms. Use the pictures below as clues.

(present tense)

1. Sue is _____.

   I am _____.

   Joe is _____.

   They are _____.

   Mary is _____.

(like)

2. I _____ to think.

   Sue _____ to swim.

   Joe _____ to eat.

   They _____ to cry.

   Mary _____ to read.

(swim)

3. They _____.

   Sue _____.

   Mary _____.

   I _____.

   Joe _____.

(want)

4. They _____ to laugh.

   Sue _____ to eat.

   Mary _____ to cry.

   I _____ to swim.

   Joe _____ to read.

5. Who is swimming? _____

   Who is crying? _____

   Who is eating? _____

   Who is reading? _____

   Who is thinking? _____

making a salad	mending a shirt with a hole and a missing button
making pizza	giving a dog a bath
	wrapping a gift and addressing it for the mail
cleaning house	painting the walls of a room

going fishing

making an
ice cream
sundae

building a
fire

making a
bed

changing
a tire

starting and
driving a car

going camping
and setting up
for the night

packing for a trip	planting a garden
	making a sandwich
setting the table	raking leaves
taking a bath	shaving your face

Aa	Bb	Cc	Dd	Ee

car

————————————————
- - - - - - - - - - -
1. a ————————————

bee

————————————————
- - - - - - - - - - -
2. ————————————————

dog

————————————————
- - - - - - - - - - -
3. ————————————————

arm

————————————————
- - - - - - - - - - -
4. ————————————————

ear

————————————————
- - - - - - - - - - -
5. ————————————————

Here are the ingredients you will need
to make brownies.

1 cup cocoa   ¾ cup flour

½ cup butter   ½ cup walnuts

1 cup sugar   1 teaspoon vanilla

2 eggs   ⅛ teaspoon salt

½ teaspoon baking powder

Now here are the instructions, but
they're all jumbled up! Find the logical
order, and write the correct number in
the blank before each step.

_____ Pour into greased pan.

_____ Butter a square pan.

_____ In a bowl, beat sugar, eggs, salt, and vanilla.

_____ Add walnuts if desired.

_____ Bake until the top is dry, about 30-35 minutes.

_____ Add flour, cocoa, and baking powder to egg mixture.

_____ Set the oven at 325°.

_____ Cool.

_____ Cut into squares.

Below is a table of equivalent mea-
sures. Can you convert the recipe into
metric measurements?

28 grams = 1 ounce	3 teaspoons = 1 tablespoon
100 grams = ¾ cup	1 ounce = 2 tablespoons
1 liter = 1 quart	8 ounces = 1 cup

a pet store

a vegetable garden

a restaurant

an amusement park

a factory

a library— inside

a dentist's office

a toy store

a bakery store window

a playground

a baseball game at a stadium

a garage in a person's home

the inside of a church

the inside of a hospital

a doctor's examining room

a bathroom

a kitchen

your bedroom

the outside of a car

a tree

the outside of a house

Directions:

Fill in the blanks in the analogy chart
below.

1. winner: loser = lucky: _____

2. friendly: unfriendly = happy: _____

3. orange: fruit = elephant: _____

4. daisy: flower = cabinet: _____

5. sofa: couch = tap: _____

6. quick: fast = pretty: _____

7. milk: bottle = bread: _____

8. teacher: teach = painter: _____

Name _____ Date _____ Activity 18

Directions:
Fill in the blanks with the correct answers.

1. I see with my _____.
   a. nose   b. eyes   c. ears   d. legs

2. I smell with my _____.
   a. feet   b. ears   c. nose   d. fingers

3. I lift with my _____.
   a. arms   b. head   c. toes   d. neck

4. I put a hat on my _____.
   a. eyes   b. nose   c. hand   d. head

5. I run with my _____.
   a. fingers   b. legs   c. hair   d. elbows

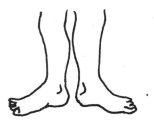

6. I comb my _____.
   a. hair   b. toes   c. stomach   d. knees

7. I write with my _____.
   a. toes   b. chest   c. fingers   d. stomach

8. I talk with my _____.
   a. mouth   b. ears   c. nose   d. eyes

Directions:

Say each word listed below, and decide if it begins with a voiced or a voiceless consonant. Write each word in the correct column.

Voiced   **Voiceless**

1. duck
2. pen
3. boat
4. table
5. garden
6. cake
7. fish
8. zero
9. seat
10. veil

Directions:
Draw a line from the name of the
object to the place you would find it.

1. apple	shoe store
2. hammer	bookstore
3. medicine	jewelry store
4. shoes	bakery
5. gasoline	drugstore
6. ring	gasoline station
7. cake	hardware store
8. books	grocery store

Name one other object that can be
found in each of the above stores.

shoe store _____

bookstore _____

jewelry store _____

bakery _____

drugstore _____

gasoline station _____

hardware store _____

grocery store _____

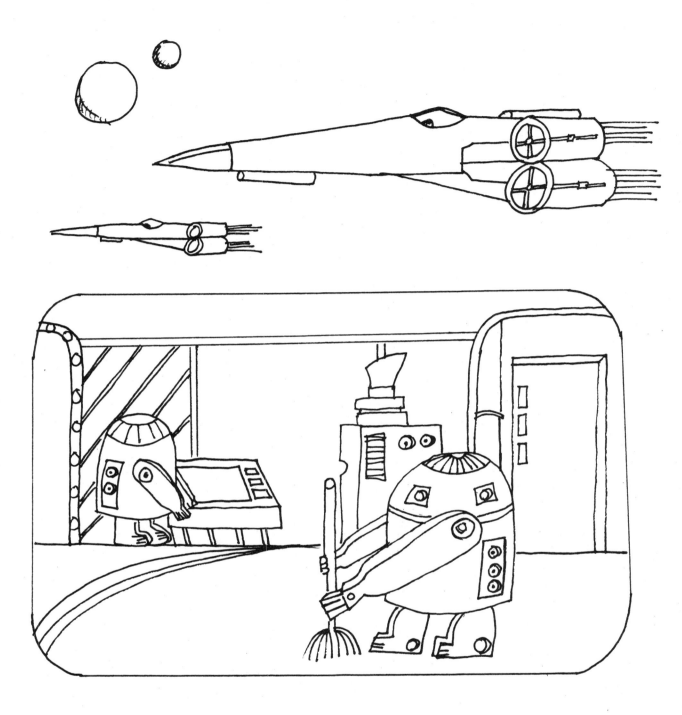

1. People drive spaceships.

2. People can live on little food.

3. People have short legs and long hands.

4. We can travel from one planet to another.

5. Robots work for people.

Directions:
Draw a human body, and label each
part with the correct word from the list
below.

head

eyes

ears

nose

mouth

neck

hair

shoulders

arms

hands

fingers

chest

stomach

legs

feet (foot)

toes

teeth (tooth)

Vegetables

		Prepositions
bean	pea	above
beet	pepper	inside
carrot	pumpkin	on
corn	tomato	on top of
lettuce	watermelon	under

1. Carrots and _____ grow _____ the ground.

2. _____ and watermelons grow _____ a vine.

3. _____ grow _____ a pod.

4. _____ grows _____ a husk.

5. Beans and _____ grow _____ the ground.

6. _____ and pumpkins grow _____ the ground.

Directions:

What do you say to these people when they come to your door? Write your answers in the spaces provided.

Little Boy: I seem to be lost. Can you help me?

You: _____

_____

_____

Lady: Please contribute to the Red Cross.

You: _____

_____

_____

Lady: Savon Cosmetics calling. Let me make you beautiful.

You: _____

_____

_____

Across:

1. The _____ greeted the pilgrims when they arrived at Plymouth Rock.

4. _____ change color every autumn before falling from the trees.

6. _____ syrup is made from the sap of the tree.

7. _____ pie is a favorite dessert on this holiday.

8. _____ is celebrated on the third Thursday of November each year.

9. The _____ left England to escape religious persecution.

Down:

2. Another name for _____ is fall.

3. _____ is the time of year when farmers gather their crops.

5. _____ have become an important part of the Thanksgiving meal.

JOAQUIN

CARMELA

ANA

CHRISTINA

PABLO

ENRIQUE

ROSALINN

Directions:

Fill in the blanks with the correct words from the vocabulary list on Worksheet D. Use the pictures on Worksheet A for help.

Example:

I AM CHRISTINA.

1. Joaquin is my <u>father</u>.

2. Carmela is my <u>sister</u>.

3. Ana is my <u>mother</u>.

4. Pablo is my <u>grandfather</u>.

5. Enrique is my <u>brother</u>.

6. Rosalinn is my <u>grandmother</u>.

CHRISTINA

I AM JOAQUIN.

1. Carmela is my _____.

2. Ana is my _____.

3. Christina is my _____.

4. Pablo is my _____.

5. Enrique is my _____.

6. Rosalinn is my _____.

JOAQUIN

I AM CARMELA.

1. Ana is my _____.

2. Christina is my _____.

3. Pablo is my _____.

4. Enrique is my _____.

5. Rosalinn is my _____.

6. Joaquin is my _____.

CARMELA

I AM ANA.

1. Christina is my _____.

2. Pablo is my _____.

3. Enrique is my _____.

4. Rosalinn is my _____.

5. Joaquin is my _____.

6. Carmela is my _____.

ANA

I AM PABLO.

1. Enrique is my _____.

2. Rosalinn is my _____.

3. Joaquin is my _____.

4. Carmela is my _____.

5. Christina is my _____.

6. Ana is my _____.

PABLO

I AM ENRIQUE.

1. Rosalinn is my _____.

2. Joaquin is my _____.

3. Carmela is my _____.

4. Christina is my _____.

5. Ana is my _____.

6. Pablo is my _____.

ENRIQUE

I AM ROSALINN.

1. Joaquin is my _____.

2. Carmela is my _____.

3. Christina is my _____.

4. Ana is my _____.

5. Pablo is my _____.

6. Enrique is my _____.

ROSALINN

Vocabulary List

mother	wife
father	husband
sister	daughter
brother	son
grandmother	granddaughter
grandfather	grandson

Name _____ Date _____ Activity 26-E

Directions:

Draw pictures of your family members
in the correct balloons.

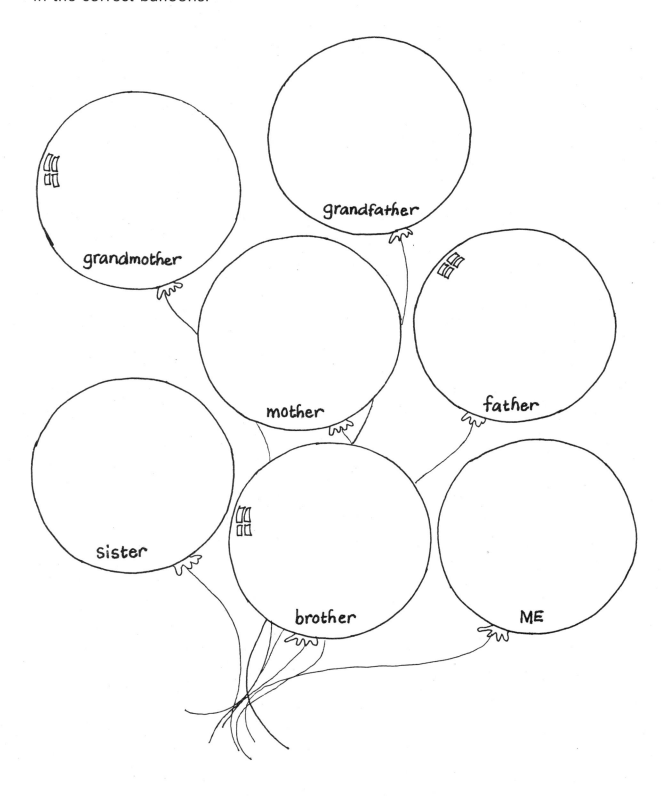

Directions:

Study the list of words below, then write each word under the correct picture. Write a short paragraph about each building, using some of the vocabulary words listed under it.

hay	tractor	cow
books	chalk	shovel
toys	pets	beds
horse	rakes	maps
television	basement	desks
couch	gym	blackboard

HOUSE   **BARN**   **SCHOOL**

Directions:
Draw a line from each mother animal
to her baby. Then cut out the names of
the animals and paste them under the
correct pictures.

dog   puppy   horse   colt   cat   kitten   pig   piglet

Directions:

Here is a list of the occupations pictured on Worksheets A and B.

cook (chef)	artist	musician
secretary	salesman (saleswoman)	architect
teacher	pilot	computer operator
actress (actor)	waiter (waitress)	doctor

In the sentences below, fill in the blanks to make each statement true. There may be more than one correct answer for each sentence.

Example: A <u>musician</u> plays music.

1. A salesman _____.

2. A waiter _____.

3. A _____ works with computers.

4. A _____ flies airplanes.

5. A teacher _____.

6. A _____ makes T.V. commercials.

7. A secretary _____.

8. A doctor _____.

9. A _____ works in a restaurant.

10. A _____ works in an office.

11. An artist _____.

12. A _____ plays in an orchestra.

13. An _____ designs buildings.

14. An _____ works in an art studio.

15. A chef _____.

16. A _____ serves food to customers.

Name _____ Date _____ Activity 30-A

Directions:

1. Find the simple past tense form of each verb listed below, and write it in the blank provided.

Example: I feel, I <u>felt</u>.

You hear   You _____

We come   We _____

I forget   I _____

We have   We _____

She buys    She _____

They go   They _____

He sees    He _____

I have   I _____

You speak   You _____

She is   She _____

They think    They _____

We tell   We _____

He eats    He _____

I know   I _____

They write    They _____

She gets   She _____

I am   I _____

We feel   We _____

2. Now, without looking at the previous exercise, identify each verb pictured below. Give the infinitive and simple past tense forms for each verb.

Example: to tell, told.

1.  _____   5.  _____

2.  _____   6.  _____

3.  _____   7.  _____

4. _____   8.  _____

1A. deep   1B. shallow   5A. empty   5B. full
2A. large   2B. small   6A. straight   6B. crooked
3A. over   3B. under   7A. fat   7B. skinny
4A. dark   4B. light   8A. happy   8B. sad

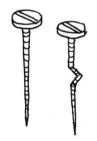

Student 1:

1. Write your name in Box 1 of the diagram.

2. Have your partner ask you questions A-E. Write your answers in the left row of boxes. (Answer each question in a complete sentence that starts with *I.*)

Student 2:

1. Write your name in Box 2 of the diagram.

2. Have your partner ask you questions A-E. Write your answers in the right row of boxes. (Answer each question in a complete sentence that starts with *I.*)

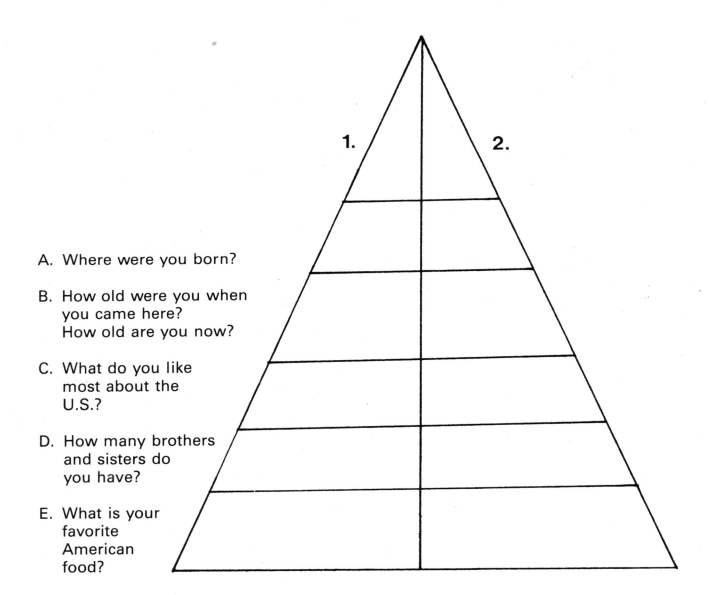

A. Where were you born?

B. How old were you when you came here?
   How old are you now?

C. What do you like most about the U.S.?

D. How many brothers and sisters do you have?

E. What is your favorite American food?

MAY	**OCTOBER**
APRIL	**JANUARY**
SEPTEMBER	**JUNE**
MARCH	**FEBRUARY**
JULY	**DECEMBER**
NOVEMBER	**AUGUST**
FALL	**WINTER**
SPRING	**SUMMER**

A HUNT

Item	**Item's use**
1. _____	_____
2. _____	_____
3. _____	_____
4. _____	_____
5. _____	_____
6. _____	_____
7. _____	_____
8. _____	_____
9. _____	_____
10. _____	_____
11. _____	_____
12. _____	_____
13. _____	_____
14. _____	_____
15. _____	_____
16. _____	_____
17. _____	_____
18. _____	_____
19. _____	_____
20. _____	_____
21. _____	_____
22. _____	_____
23. _____	_____
24. _____	_____
25. _____	_____

Directions:

This is Mr. Jones. Can you name all his parts? Fill in the blanks with the correct parts of the body.

1. running   2. sleeping   3. eating   4. climbing   5. jumping

A. He (1) _____

B. They (2) _____

C. She (4) _____

D. The monkey and the bird (4) _____

E. You (3) _____

F. The kangaroo (5) _____

G. We (1) _____

H. All of the clowns (2) _____

I. I (3) _____

J. None of the dogs (2) _____

K. The men (1) _____

L. The little girl (5) _____

M. You and I (4) _____

Everyone is wearing glasses.

Most people are wearing glasses.

Some people are wearing glasses.

No one is wearing glasses.

1. Do you like the color blue?

2. Do you walk to class every day?

3. Are you a good cook?

4. Do you like football?

5. Can you dance?

6. Can you speak French?

7. Do you have a motorcycle?

8. Can you speak Japanese?

9. Do you have a dog?

10. Are you married?

11. Do you like coffee?

12. Can you swim?

13. Do you study English every day?

14. Is your birthday in July?

15. Are you going shopping after class?

16. Do you like pizza?

17. Are you young?

18. Are you old?

ARE	**GOING**
WHERE	**YOU**
WHEN	**IS**
HE	**I**
AM	**FISHING**
DOING	**WHAT**
YOUR	**NAME**
RUNNING	**WHO**

PEOPLE'S PLUS MONEY MARKET ACCOUNT RECEIPT

people's bank

ACCOUNT #

DATE	WITHDRAWAL	DEPOSIT	BALANCE	TELLER

- This PMA counter receipt is for your use as a handy record of your transactions. Keep this receipt until you receive your next monthly statement.
- Please note: this is *not* a passbook, and it is not necessary that you use it.
- Each month you will receive a statement of all activity on your PMA, *including interest earned*, which is paid the last day of every month.

Thank you for your DEPOSIT

TO ACCOUNT NO._____

ON_____   **people's bank**
       Date

TYPE OF DEPOSIT:
☐ Savings   ☐ Money Mkt.   ☐ Investments

BY _____
          Name on Account

_____
          Address

PLEASE ENDORSE ALL CHECKS	DOLLARS	CENTS
BILLS/COIN		
CHECKS (LIST EACH ITEM)		
TOTAL ITEMS		
LESS CASH RETURNED		
TOTAL DEPOSIT		

Checks and other items are received for deposit subject to verification and collection.

WITHDRAWAL
(Counter Use Only)

WITHDRAWAL (Counter Use Only)

_____19_____   Account Number _____
Date

Received from People's Bank. . .   Amount $ _____

_____Dollars

please write amount here

Please sign _____

If this withdrawal from my account is paid by check or draft, I agree to accept said check or draft as full payment for the amount of said withdrawal.

people's bank

Juanita and Pedro need to go to many different places. How can they get to each place?

Directions:

Match the pictures with the apologies listed below. Write the correct number in each blank.

_____ Can you ever forgive me, dar-
ling?

_____ I'm sorry to keep you waiting.

_____ I'm sorry, but I have to leave
now.

_____ Excuse me. May I speak with you
for a moment?

The sky is cloudy. Pepe walks home. He is walking fast. A black car stops. Pepe is afraid. He sees an open door. He runs in the door. The car stops again. Pepe goes to the window. He looks out the window. Two men get out of the car. Pepe sees a box. He hides in the box.

My name is Pepe.

The sky is cloudy.

Pepe walks fast.

A car stops.

Pepe is afraid.

The door is open.

Pepe looks out the window.

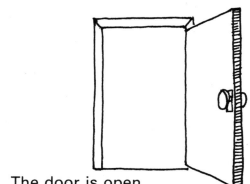

Two men get out of the car.

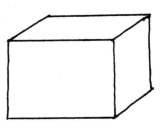

Pepe sees a box.

Directions:
Answer each question in a complete
sentence.

1. Where is Pepe walking? _____

   _____

2. Is the sky sunny? _____

3. What color is the car? _____

Answer these questions according to
the pictures on Worksheet B.

What happens first? _____

What happens second? _____

What happens third? _____

What happens fourth? _____

What happens fifth? _____

What happens sixth? _____

What happens seventh? _____

What happens eighth? _____

Write a paragraph that tells what happens to Pepe next.

_____

_____

_____

_____

_____

Name ______________________ Date ______________ Activity 44

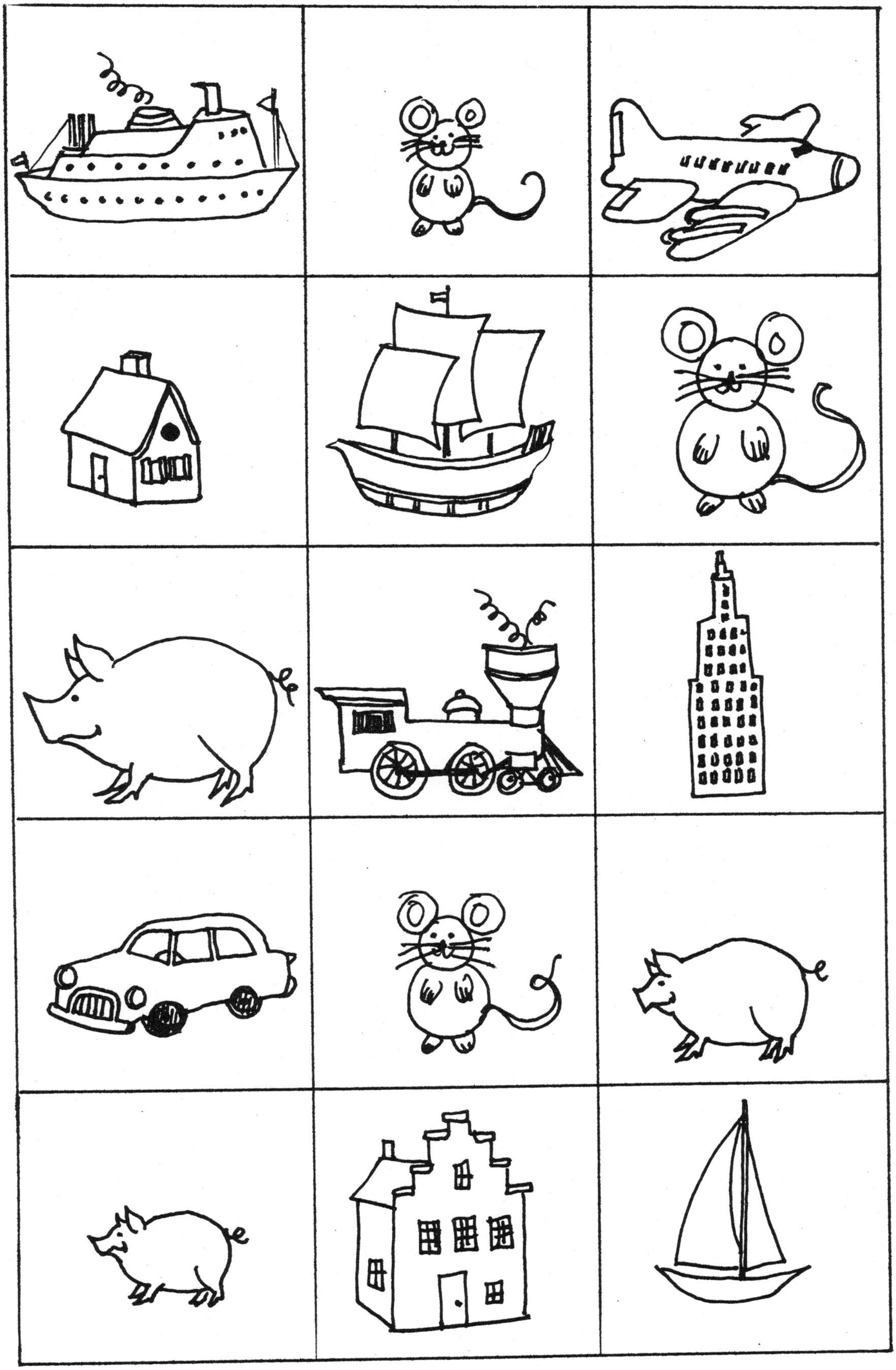

A JOB INTERVIEW

Receptionist: **May I help you?**

Applicant: I have an appointment with Mr. Worth.

Receptionist: Please have a seat . . . You may go back to Mr. Worth's office now.

Applicant: (knock, knock)

Interviewer: Come in.

Applicant: Hello, Mr. Worth, my name is _____.

Interviewer: Hello, have a seat. **What job are you applying for?**

Applicant: I want a position as a cook.

Interviewer: **Tell me about your experience in this type of work.**

Applicant: I have six years of experience. I have worked in two different restaurants. Both restaurants were famous for their fine food and service.

Interviewer: **Why should I give you a job?**

Applicant: I am an excellent cook. I have good references. I work hard, and I am responsible and dependable.

Interviewer: **Why did you leave your last job?**

Applicant: My family and I moved to the United States.

Interviewer: I pay my cooks $10 an hour.

Applicant: That sounds good.

Interviewer: You may have the job.

Applicant: Thank you very much. When may I begin?

Interviewer: Next Monday.

Applicant: Thank you very much. Good-bye.

Directions:

Label each fruit pictured below with a
word from this list.

strawberries   apple

orange   watermelon

pear   grapes

1.	2.	3.
4.	5.	6.

Questions:

1. Which fruits are grown on trees? _____

_____

2. Which fruits are grown on land? _____

_____

3. Which is your favorite fruit? Why? _____

_____

4. Which fruits are grown in the United States? _____

_____

DATE DUE

DATE DUE

OCT	NOV 1 2 1996		
Nov	JAN 0 4 1997		
JAN			
FEB 0 3			
APR	MAY 1 4 1997		
MAY 0			
MAY 3	OCT 1 6 1997		
OC	OCT 0 4 1998		
	JUN 2 3 1999		
MAY	JAN 2 4 2001		
AU			
AP			

Demco, Inc. 38-293

Demco, Inc. 38-293